APPLE WATCH 2018: 2 IN 1: YOUR ESSENTIAL APPLE WATCH RESOURCE

© Copyright 2018 by _____ - All rights reserved.

The following book is reproduced below with the goal of providing information that is as accurate and reliable as possible. Regardless, purchasing this book can be seen as consent to the fact that both the publisher and the author of this book are in no way experts on the topics discussed within and that any recommendations or suggestions that are made herein are for entertainment purposes only. Professionals should be consulted as needed prior to undertaking any of the action endorsed herein.

This declaration is deemed fair and valid by both the American Bar Association and the Committee of Publishers Association and is legally binding throughout the United States.

Furthermore, the transmission, duplication or reproduction of any of the following work including specific information will be considered an illegal act irrespective of if it is done electronically or in print. This extends to creating a secondary or tertiary copy of the work or a recorded copy and is only allowed with an expressed written consent from the Publisher. All additional rights reserved.

The information in the following pages is broadly considered to be truthful and accurate account of facts, and as such any inattention, use or misuse of the information in question by the reader will render any resulting actions solely under their purview. There are no scenarios in which the publisher or the original author of this work can be in any fashion deemed liable for any hardship or damages that may befall them after undertaking information described herein.

Additionally, the information in the following pages is intended only for informational purposes and should thus be thought of as universal. As befitting its nature, it is presented without assurance regarding its prolonged validity or interim quality. Trademarks that are mentioned are done without written consent and can in no way be considered an endorsement from the trademark holder.

Table of Contents

APPLE WATCH 2018 EDITION

Introduction 3

Part I: Purchasing the Right Apple Watch Series 3 for You 5

Part II: Using Your Apple Watch Series 3 17

Part III: Personalizing Your Apple Watch Series 3 31

Part IV: Tips & Tricks 43

Conclusion 51

APPLE WATCH: 101 Helpful Tips and Secret Tricks

Introduction 57

Chapter 1: Getting to Know Your Apple Watch Series 3 59

Chapter 2: Maximizing Apple Watch Performance 69

Chapter 3: Navigation & Notifications 79

Chapter 4: Hack Your Life: How to Utilize Apple Watch Series 3 to Improve Time Management, Fitness, and Self-improvement 89

Chapter 5: Customization: How to Make Apple Watch Reflect Your Style and Personality 103

Chapter 6: Have More Fun: Personal Communication & Entertainment On-The-Go 111

Conclusion 119

APPLE WATCH 2018 EDITION

The Answer to All Your Series 3 Questions

Introduction

With the vision of creating an all-inclusive, touchable, and wearable computing device, Apple debuted their Apple Watch, Apple's take on the ever more popular smartwatch, in the latter months of 2016. Aesthetically pleasing as most Apple products are, the Apple Watch, at the time, offered users a stylish and functional alternative to the traditional watch.

Not only could Apple's first timepiece tell, as you might imagine, time, it could also make and take calls, send and receive texts, track your workouts, operate most social media apps, and much more. However, the Apple Watch was merely a pretty accessory, redundant in terms of its functions. What could the watch do that the phone could not? Furthermore, the Apple Watch most notably lacked cellular connectivity, essentially hinging the functionality of the timepiece to its owner's iPhone.

In other words, if your iPhone runs out of battery, your Apple Watch Series 1 or 2, due to its lack of cellular connection, would not be able to receive calls, rendering the timepiece more of a cosmetic extension to the iPhone than an effective standalone device. Users needed to bring both their watch and iPhone with them to get any use out of the former. So, Apple went back to the drawing board, trying to design a smartwatch that would allow its users to leave the phone at home and bring just the timepiece.

Released in September 2017, the Apple Watch Series 3 marked Apple's fix to the problem of redundancy: add cellular connectivity to the newest Apple Watch, providing users with the option to leave their phones at home and simply wear the smartwatch out. So, what majorly differentiates the Apple Watch Series 3 from its predecessors is its LTE cellular connectivity, represented by the striking red digital crown on the right side of the watch face. Users do not need to carry their phones around because the Apple Watch Series 3 has its own functioning cellular connection. Also, with the S3 chip, an upgrade to the Series 3, the user will experience a much-improved responsiveness to the device in comparison to previous models. Thus, the Apple Watch Series 3 is an upgrade on its predecessors in both processing speed and its ability to standalone from the user's mobile device.

Having established the basic background information for the Apple Watch Series 3, this book will guide you on how to get the most out of your timepiece, whether it be aesthetically or functionally. The Apple Watch perfectly intersects style and utility, so why not optimize both? What will follow is three parts: a buyer's guide on assembling the watch that you want; a tutorial on how to operate the watch and its major apps; and how to personalize the functions of the watch.

Part I
Purchasing the Right Apple Watch Series 3 for You

When it comes to purchasing the right Apple Watch Series 3, the ostensibly limitless customization options can cause much hesitation and doubt. What band should I buy? What color case should I buy? How much will it all cost? There's no need to stress and research your options for hours—just peruse the comprehensive overview of the choices available to you below.

1. General Specifications (from Apple website)

Series 3 (GPS) Features

- Built-in GPS and GLONASS
- Faster dual-core processor
- W2 chip
- Barometric altimeter
- Capacity 8GB
- Heart rate sensor
- Accelerometer and gyroscope
- Water resistant 50 meters

- Ion-X strengthened glass
- Composite back
- Wi-Fi (802.11b/g/n 2.4GHz)
- Bluetooth 4.2
- Up to 18 hours of battery life3
- Watch OS 4

Series 3 (GPS + Cellular) Features

- Built-in GPS and GLONASS
- Faster dual-core processor
- W2 chip
- Barometric altimeter
- Capacity 16GB
- Heart rate sensor
- Accelerometer and gyroscope
- Water resistant 50 meters
- Ion-X strengthened glass
- Ceramic back
- Wi-Fi (802.11b/g/n 2.4GHz)

- Bluetooth 4.2
- Up to 18 hours of battery life
- Watch OS 4

A Few Definitions

The following are definitions for some of the terms listed above so that the layman can understand precisely what the Series 3 offers.

GLONASS - An acronym for Global Navigation Satellite System, GLONASS was developed in Russia. It was the Soviet Union's answer to the United States' widely known GPS. GLONASS alone does not provide the strength of coverage that GPS does; nevertheless, the Russian technology thrives in its accuracy and capacity to track you between skyscrapers and subways—two areas which GPS cannot cover. So, with the Series 3, you get a device that has both GLONASS and GPS, allowing for the great coverage wherever you are going.

W2 Chip - According to Apple, the W2 chip—an upgrade from the W1 chip—delivers boosted Wi-Fi speeds and makes the watch more power efficient when using Bluetooth and Wi-Fi in comparison to the previous generations of the Apple Watch. Ultimately, the W2 chip renders the Series 3 a more efficient device than the Series

1 or 2, addressing possible battery life issues users might have.

Barometric Altimeter - New to the Apple Watch Series 3, the barometric altimeter allows the watch to track elevation in your workouts. The barometric altimeter basically assesses how altitude affects your body during your exercises.

Accelerometer and gyroscope - Both are sensors that track and record motion data. Getting reads on your sleep patterns, your heartrate, your breathing are all done by these sensors.

Ion-X Strengthened Glass - Apple's scratch-resistant technology used for their Apple Watch displays. This is their alternative to the traditional sapphire glass often used for regular watch faces.

2. LTE Cellular vs. Non-Cellular/GPS-only

As stated in the introduction, Apple differentiated the Apple Watch Series 3 from its predecessors by incorporating LTE cellular connectivity to the device. That being said, Apple does offer the Series 3 in a non-cellular option; however, going with this option brings back the redundancy issue. But, it is not only in cellular connectivity that these two options differ. The LTE Cellular Series 3 has 16GB of storage to the Non-cellular's 8GB; the LTE Cellular Series 3 offers many more casing options while the Non-Cellular is restricted to aluminum casings; the battery life averages about 18 hours of use for both. Nevertheless, if you are an individual who likes to have their phone always on hand, then, perhaps, the non-cellular Series 3 would be the best choice for you.

After deciding on whether you want cellular connectivity or not, you simply need to choose what watch size you want. Both the Cellular and Non-cellular versions come in 38mm and 42mm. The thing to take into account here is, if you want a Hermes watch single or double tour watch band, each only fits on one size.

3. Casing Options

For the GPS-only version of the Series 3, the casing options are quite limited—in actuality, aluminum is the only available casing material for the Non-cellular watch. Given that, you do get to choose the color of the casing, but even that choice is restricted to silver, gold, and space gray (a dark grey verging on black). GPS-only Series 3 watches go for $329.

The Cellular Series 3 gives a few more options in regards to casing material:

For the buyer looking for the cheapest option, Apple offers the Cellular Series 3 in the aluminum casings that are used for the GPS-only Series 3. These casings come in the same colors as the Non-cellular casings. The Cellular

Series 3 goes for $399 in the aluminum casing, $70 more than the GPS-only version.

The second option, the mid-price casing material, is stainless steel. This casing material comes in a glossy, metallic silver color or space grey. The stainless steel casing proves much more resilient than the aluminum casing, providing a "diamond-like carbon" (DLC) coating. This casing material is the most reminiscent of traditional timepieces, with its classic and abiding style and strength.

The 'high-end' option is the ceramic casing option. While the ceramic casing is even harder than steel, it is also more prone to shattering on a hard surface than the stainless-steel casing is. In essence, the ceramic casing is the most scratch-resistant out of the three options, but it is not as robust a material as stainless steel. The casing comes in two simple color options: white or black. Ceramic Series 3 models begin at $1299, quite a significant increase in price from the stainless steel option.

4. Band Options

Again, just like with the casing options for the Series 3 GPS-only watch, the band options are quite limited. The first option is the sport band, which comes in the colors fog (a light grey color), pink sand (a cream pink color), space gray, and black. The sport band is composed of fluoroelastomer, a synthetic rubber that resists most chemicals. The second options is the Nike + sport band, which is composed of fluoroelastomer as well, but comes in the pure platinum (white) and the anthracite colors. The difference between the two bands is purely cosmetic, both priced at the same value. The normal sport band is quite plain while the Nike + sport band comes covered with little holes, allowing for breathability.

The band options for the Series 3 Cellular do not leave much to be desired. However, depending on the casing you purchase, your band options may be more or less limited, still. If desired, you can purchase the normal sport band or Nike + sport band with all three casings. The Series 3 Cellular does have alternative cheap options: the sport loop and the Nike + sport loop. The sport loop is made of a nylon material and comes in black, seashell (a silver color), and pink sand. The Nike + sport loop comes in midnight fog (a grey green color) and black/platinum. The only difference between the normal sport loop and the Nike + sport loop is the available colors. So, for the aluminum version of the Series 3 Cellular, the sport bands and sport loops are your options.

The stainless steel casing has the most band options available. As stated before, the sport bands and loops can be purchased with the stainless steel casing, but for those looking for more expensive bands, the Milanese loop is another option. The Milanese loop, a stainless steel mesh developed in Italy, allows for the user to find a personalized fit for their watch because of its magnetic properties. In other words, the Milanese loop is infinitely adjustable. Series 3 watches that come with the Milanese loop start at $699. If you want the watch with the space grey Milanese loop, then the price increases to $749. Furthermore, the stainless steel casing has the Hermes—the French luxury goods manufacturer—collaboration option. The Hermes bands offer a leather alternative, bringing a classic, traditional look to Apple's smartwatch. The single tour option, for the most part, can only be paired with the 42mm size casing; the double tour option with the 38mm size casing. There are a few exceptions to the single tour band, allowing it to be compatible with both casing sizes. The two main colors for the Hermes bands are fauve and indigo, and the stainless steel Series 3 with the Hermes band starts at $1299.

The options for the ceramic casing are even more limited than the band options for the aluminum casing. Nevertheless, the sport band that comes with the ceramic casing comes with ceramic accents while the aluminum sport band only has aluminum accents. The color options are black and white.

> Note: Only the sport band and sport loop are water-resistant. So, these bands would be best for those who want to exercise while wearing the Series 3.

What should be known is that third-party companies have designed their own bands. The information provided above covers the factory options Apple offers on its website. If none of the options sound particularly appealing to you, the bands, out of all the physical components of the Series 3, is the easiest to customize. A search on the internet will bring up a profusion of alternative options not offered by Apple. Undoubtedly, most people will be able to find some band design they like, even if it is not sold by a company other than Apple.

Simplifying the Choice

To simplify your choice, this is a distillation of the information covered in this section:

- Decide whether you want cellular connectivity or not. Granted, LTE Cellular is the main innovation of the Apple Watch Series 3, but if you do not mind the watch's functionality being tethered to your iPhone, then there is no need to pay the upcharge. Furthermore, you should know that, to even use cellular on your watch, you need to sign up for a plan with a provider such as AT&T. This will, of course, incur a monthly cost of ~$10.

- Take into consideration that Cellular vs. Non-Cellular is not the only differentiating factor between the two versions of the Series 3. The Series 3 Cellular comes with double the storage, a plethora of stock band options, and a ceramic back. The Series 3 GPS-only comes with a composite back, making the underside of the watch more prone to scratching and breakage in comparison to the Series 3 Cellular's back.

- Aluminum casings, while the cheapest option, are not particularly resilient. Scratches will easily show on your casing. Also, the aluminum casing does not come with as many band options as the stainless steel casing does. That being said, the aluminum casing is also the lightest material out of the three casing variations. This casing could be best for athletes or those living an active lifestyle as it is lightweight but also the most affordable to replace out of the three casings. You will not feel weighed down or have to constantly worry about damaging one of the more expensive casings if you go for the aluminum option. The aluminum Series

3 is also the best entry point for those who want to try out Apple's timepiece without having to break the bank, per say. Series 3 GPS-only costs $329; Series 3 Cellular prices costs $399.

- Stainless steel casings and the mid-range option in price, is resilient but not as scratchproof as the ceramic casing. If you have no interest in buying a band from a third-party seller, then the stainless steel Series 3 has the most stock band options available, ranging from the sport band to the supple leather Hermes bands. The stainless steel casing also delivers a classic look as it is a material often used for traditional, luxury timepieces. Thus, the stainless steel Series 3 fuses timeless style and modern technology that want a sophisticated workhorse. You will not have the worry about breakage with the stainless steel casing whatsoever. Stainless steel Series 3 prices start at $599 and can, when packaged with one of the Hermes bands, go for up to $1299.

- Ceramic casings, the unique but pricey option, will distinguish you from everyone else in the sea of Apple Watch wearers, but only for the price of $1299. The band options are the most limited out of all the three's, but the ceramic casing, while not as resilient as the stainless steel casing, is the most scratch-resistant.

- Keep in mind, as well, that the limited stock band options for each casing should be the least of your concerns. You can always search for one that is offered by a third-party seller and switch it out with the one that comes packaged with your Series 3.

Part II
Using Your Apple Watch Series 3

Controlling the Apple Watch

As far as interacting or physically operating the Apple Watch Series 3 goes, the controls are quite simple. Looking at the picture above, you see the three main components that the user needs to utilize their watch: the watch face, the dial/digital crown, and the side button.

1. The Watch Face

Akin to most smart devices, the watch face is operated by touch. To make full use of the Series 3, the user must familiarize themselves with four gestures/actions.

1. Tap—action used to select buttons on the display and "wake up" the display.

2. Press or "Force touch"—action that allows user to go to options in apps and change the look of their watch face.

3. Drag—action that involves keeping the finger on the display and scrolling or adjusting sliders. For example, the drag gesture is used to navigate the Maps app because you may need to adjust what part of the map you want to look at on the screen.

4. Swipe—action that can be performed in all four directions (up, down, left, and right) and involves a quick swipe of the finger on the display.

2. The Dial/Digital Crown

Again, the red coloration of this component clearly differentiates the Series 3 Cellular and the GPS-only versions. Nevertheless, the digital crown functions the same way for both. Two actions can be performed using the digital crown: press and rotate. The press gesture can, depending on the number and length of presses, result in different commands.

1. Short press—returns the user to the home screen, which can be the user's personalized watch screen.

2. Press and hold—triggers Siri, Apple's AI that can perform basic tasks such as a Google search for the user.

3. Double-click/double-press—returns the user to the last used application.

4. Rotate—rotating the digital crown can zoom, scroll, or adjust what it is on the screen.

5. Slow rotation when watch screen is off—this action will gradually increase or decrease the brightness of the display.

3. The Side Button

The side button—the oval shaped button under the digital crown—is the third component necessary for operating your Apple Watch Series 3. As you might expect, the user must press the side button for it to work, but depending on the number and length of presses, different commands will be triggered.

1. Short press—shows or hides the Dock (a scrolling page of the user's favorite/most-used apps, more on this later).

2. Long press and hold—gives user the option to send out a SOS, but also just works to turn the device on and off.

3. Double-click/double-press—starts the Apple Pay application.

How to use the Main Applications/Features

The Apple Watch Series 3 - at least, the Cellular version - is meant to provide the same service and features as the iPhone does. Apple includes the essentials in the watch, allowing users to leave their phone at home.

1. Siri

Siri is Apple's "Intelligent Assistant," which will help you navigate your Apple Watch. You can activate her by pressing and holding the digital crown or saying "Hey, Siri." Siri offers the easiest way of getting to the exact app you want to use without having to use your hands.

2. Home Screen

The Home Screen is the "page," which displays all of the apps you have downloaded on your Apple Watch. To get to the Home Screen, you simply press the digital crown once. The total number of apps you have on the watch is completely up to you—or in some cases, depends on how much storage you have. There are two options available for the look of the Home Screen: honeycomb and list.

i. Honeycomb

Intended to loosely mimic the appearance of a honeycomb, this default option is aesthetically pleasing. However, the more apps you have, the more cluttered the Home Screen looks, making navigating the screen more difficult. Here, the rotation function on the digital crown comes in handy as you can zoom in and zoom out of the page, allowing you to see more or fewer apps depending on how close or far you have set the zoom.

If you would like to rearrange your apps, you force touch one of your apps, causing all of them to jiggle. You can now drag your apps around so that they are configured the way you want them to be. Force touching also allows you to remove an app from your watch completely. This will not delete the corresponding app on your iPhone, though.

ii. List

The more functional option of the two, the list view is as simple as it sounds. Your Home Screen will simply be a list of your apps. Considering the functionality of the Dock - more on this next - the Home Screen may not even be a feature that you frequently use. Nevertheless, the list may not be visually attractive, but it gets the job done.

> Tip: Rather than use the Home Screen, Siri seems to be the most effective and expedient option to navigating the Apple Watch Series 3. Just press and hold the digital crown to activate her.

3. The Dock

What is the Dock? Well, it is a list of your favorite applications. You can swipe or scroll through miniature "pages" or snapshots of your most-used apps. If you want to add an app to your dock, you start up whatever application it is and then press the side button. A button asking you whether you want to keep the app in the Dock will appear, and you just tap the button if you do. If you wish to remove an application from your Dock, you press the side button, scroll to the app, and swipe up. The option to remove the app from your Dock should appear as an X symbol. In essence, the Dock serves as the quickest method to get to the apps you use the most.

4. The Control Center

Just like the iPhone's Control Center, the Apple Watch Series 3 has its own simplified version. The Control Center gives you quick and easy access to the essential settings of the watch. To get to the Control Center, you simply swipe up from the main watch face screen, revealing the hidden page. The Control Center shows you how much battery life you have left, allows you to connect to your Bluetooth headphones, turn the watch into a flashlight, silence the watch, and turn on airplane mode. If you purchased the Cellular version, the Wi-Fi and Cellular Data buttons will also be found in the Control Center.

> Tip: If you are using the Apple AirPods, checking the battery life of the watch will also show you the battery life of your AirPods. There is also the battery saver option if you check your battery life.

5. Making and Taking Calls

Probably one of, if not the most, important features of a phone is the ability to call—isn't that the point of a phone? Of course, for most modern consumers, the whole process of making and taking calls comes as second nature, so it should be pretty intuitive with the Apple Watch, as well.

When someone is calling you, the number appears on your display, giving you the option of accepting or rejecting the call with the tap gesture. If you swipe up, the Apple Watch gives you the option to reject with a text message or answer the call on your iPhone. The Series 3 does not have an audio jack, meaning you must have Bluetooth headphones/earbuds unless you are fine with your conversation being public. When in the call, the volume control appears as a slider at the top of the display. To adjust the volume you can just tap the + or − sign depending on your preferences.

Making calls is harder than taking one. The best way to make a phone call is to press and hold the digital crown in order to trigger Siri. You can just dictate the number or the name (if the individual is in your friends/contacts list) to her. Another method to phone people is to use the Phone app. Your Apple Watch should be synced to your iPhone, so all of your contacts should be present in the timepiece. You simply start the Phone app and scroll through your contacts—pretty self-explanatory.

6. Messages

Similarly to making a call, the easiest way to send a text would be through Siri. A command such as "Siri, I want to send a text to X" works. Otherwise, you can manually go to the Message app on the Series 3 through the Dock or the Home Screen. After selecting the chat or person you want to message, you have three options: dictation; emoji; and digital touch.

Dictation, as the denotation of the word suggests, is when you speak into your watch, and it will record and transcribe your message into text form. Remember that you need to say the punctuation you want in your sentence. For example, if you want to end your sentence with a period, you need to dictate "period."

The emoji message gives you the option to send any kind of emoji from Apple's extensive catalogue to your recipient. Perhaps, the most interesting messaging option is the Series 3's digital touch feature.

Digital touch allows the you to send an image sketched on the screen, taps, kisses (tap two fingers on screen one or more times), your heartbeat (place two fingers on screen until you feel your heartbeat and see a visual of a heart), a broken heart (swipe down after copying the process to get your heartbeat, and anger (touch and hold one finger on the screen). You can change the colors of all these visuals by tapping the circle in the top right of the display.

Currently, the Apple Watch Series 3 does not have the capability to send images. You can, however, transfer your photos from your iPhone to your Apple Watch, so you can view your pictures on the timepiece. You can also receive photos from others through messages, as well.

7. Notifications

Notifications are the exact same as the ones you receive on your smartphone. They can range from text messages to tweets to news alerts. Just apply the same alert/notification feed you have on your phone, and that is what you get on the Apple Watch. Notifications will go directly to your timepiece when your iPhone is locked.

When you receive a notification, swipe left to get the option to delete it, tap on it to get all of the text, and clear all by force touching. To regulate what notifications you want on your watch, you need to use the My Watch app on your iPhone and decide which apps you would like notifications from.

8. Maps and Directions

Just like with all the other applications, you can access the Maps app by activating Siri, finding it on your Home Screen, or going to your Dock, if you have added the Maps app to it. Also, the Maps app will start if you click on an address in a text or email.

After starting the Maps app, you need to tap the My Location button. This will take you to your location on the digital map. From here, you can rotate the digital crown to zoom in or zoom out from where you currently are. Alternatively, you can simply use the drag gesture to manually control what part of the map is on the display. To return to the main screen, hit the back arrow at the top left.

If you are looking for directions to a specific place or just nearby shopping, dining, gas, etc. locations, you can start the search from the main menu of the Maps app. After deciding on where you intend to go, the Apple Watch will give you the choice of walking, driving, or public transport directions. Twelve steady vibrations means that you will need to turn right; three pairs of two vibrations means that you will need to turn left. The Apple Watch alerts you that you are near your destination with vibrations, as well.

At the top left, you have the option to either see the estimated time of arrival or the amount of time left to get to your destination. You can toggle between the two by simply tapping the top left.

If you want to stop receiving directions, you need to force touch the screen. The Stop Directions button will pop up as a circle with an x in the middle. Perhaps, if you have a good idea of how to get to your destination, you should stop receiving directions in order to conserve your battery, especially when you have left your iPhone at home.

> Tip: If you tend to use a certain mode of transportation, you can set a default from the My Watch app on your iPhone

9. Viewing Reminders and the Calendar app

In order to use the Calendar app on the Series 3, you need to have it first set up on an iPhone. Your Calendar app can be synced with Google Calendar, Facebook, Exchange, Yahoo, and some other services. As with all other applications, there are multiple methods to getting to your Calendar app—Siri, putting it in the Dock, going through the Home Screen. As far as scheduling events, that would be best done through your iPhone rather than the Series 3. When in the Calendar app on your watch, you can toggle between the List view (for those who want to see everything they have to do that day) and the Up Next view (for those who just want to know what is up next on their schedule). You can change your view by force touching the display; this will bring up the two variations.

Reminders are just another form of notification, so what was written in the notification setting applies to reminders, as well. The best way to customize your reminder settings is through the My Watch app on your iPhone. Just know, there is no dedicated Reminders app on the Apple Watch

Series 3, but that does not mean you do not have the ability to set up a reminder. You will have to utilize Siri—your assistant—to make a reminder for yourself. Tell her what you need to be reminded of and when you need to be reminded.

10. Weather app

As you would expect, the Apple Watch Series 3 also gives you information on the weather. You can see upcoming weather patterns by manually going to the app or by asking Siri. The Weather app informs you of the temperature, conditions, and chance of rain. The location(s) displayed on the Weather app on your watch will reflect those on your iPhone, so if you need to add or delete any locale, you will need to do that on the iPhone's Weather app.

Part III
Personalizing Your Apple Watch Series 3

So you have chosen the right Series 3 watch for you and now know how to operate it, but you want to make the timepiece feel like it is really yours. Throughout this book, some ways of personalizing the experiences have already been mentioned, such as deciding on the honeycomb or list view for your Home Screen and controlling what you want in your Dock. This section will get into the minutiae of the experience so that you can tailor your watch to your exact needs and desires.

1. **Watch Face Design**

To change the watch face design, you first need to press the digital crown to go to your watch face. Then, perform the force touch action to view the sundry designs available. You see them by swiping left or right, and most are customizable. Listed below is a selection of the best watch face designs:

<u>The Siri watch face</u> - The Siri watch face provides, perhaps, the most functional design. On a single page, the Siri watch face displays pertinent information to your day, whether it be an event you scheduled on your calendar or the ETA to your destination. This watch face collates what you may

need to know and organizes it into small bubbles that you can scroll through with the digital crown or by using the drag action. You can tap a bubble to see more information about the weather, to bring up the Maps app if you have started the direction service, etc. While not the most visually appealing watch face, the Siri face proves the most useful.

The kaleidoscope watch face - Making use of an image of your choice, the kaleidoscope watch face transforms a photograph into a pattern you would see when looking through a kaleidoscope. This watch face offers infinite possibilities as the pattern and colors will change depending on what image you select. Furthermore, if you want a unique watch face, then this would be best achieved through this watch face design as you can use photos that may be yours alone.

The photo watch face - Maybe, you are not taken by any of Apple's watch face offerings or you are simply bored of them. In this case, you can set one of your own photos as the watch face. Start the Photos app on your iPhone, select the picture you want as your watch face design, tap the Share icon and choose Create Watch Face. Here, you have the choice between the photo watch face or the kaleidoscope watch face. The change should immediately reflect on your Apple Watch's watch face.

The Activity digital face - A watch face best used when working out, the Activity watch face is linked to the Activity app, a fitness tracker. The app depicts three circles. On the outer rim, the pink circle displays how many calories you have burned; the middle circle, a green color, the number of minutes of exercise you have tracked; the innermost circle—blue—shows the amount of time you have stood up. The circles will be incomplete if you do not achieve your fitness goals for the day.

The utility watch face - The utility watch face recreates the look of a traditional watch face. It simply has the face of the usual analog watch—the time displayed with the hour, minute, second hands over a circle with the numbers 1-12 at the perimeter. As the name implies, this watch face is intended to cater to the utilitarian. This watch face does display a small version of the Activity app at the top right of the screen.

The modular watch face - Within the same vein as the utility and Siri watch faces, the modular face is all about giving you the information you need on one single page. From the weather to directions, this watch face can keep you informed with what is pertinent to you. This design will keep you from having to look at your phone. A simple design, the modular face looks like a busier digital watch face.

The motion watch face - this watch face breathes life into an otherwise static display. You can have a flower or a jellyfish on the screen, for example. You will not get much functionality out of this watch face design; nevertheless, you will have a pleasing visual without the inundation of notifications, alerts, and information on your screen every time you look at your Series 3. With this watch face design, you will get the time and date.

The astronomy watch face - Offered in Moon and Earth variants, the astronomy face allows you to interact with space. Rotating the digital crown can move time backwards or forwards engendering neighboring planets to spin and move. Pressing the digital crown returns the planets back to the current time. Another fun feature of this watch face is that tapping the Moon shows you the current lunar phase and rotating the digital crown displays future and past phases. Like the motion face, the astronomy face is not for those looking for the most utility out of their watch face. If you want to look at an uncluttered and aesthetically pleasing watch face and do not mind taking a few more steps to see your pertinent information, then this watch face is for you.

The chronograph watch face - The closest thing to the classic chronograph watch face, the chronograph face for the Series 3 is what its name suggests: it is a chronograph face. Those who want their Series 3 look as much like a traditional, luxury watch should consider this watch face. There are no frills or complications.

The Mickey/Minnie watch face - Are you a Disney fan? Or just a fan of Mickey and/or Minnie? Well, you are in luck. Apple offers a Mickey/Minnie watch face. You can choose between either of the characters by customizing the watch face. Whichever one you pick, he/she will say the time if you tap the display.

Customizing watch faces

Now, to get the watch face to display exactly the way you want it to, you need to force touch the display and then tap Customize. You will be able to tap the various 'complications' and/or pieces of information and use the digital crown to see the other options available to you. Simply press the digital crown after you are happy with the customizations you have made.

You can go about adding more complications and information to your Series 3 by going to your Apple Watch app on your iPhone. There should be a Complications section under the My Watch tab. Add a complication with the + button, remove a complication with the – button. Simple as that.

1. The Activity app

The pre-installed Activity app is Apple's fitness tracker and motivator. Essentially, you set an exercise or "move" goal, which is the amount of calories you would like to burn on a daily basis. You can set your move goal by launching the Activity app and force touching the screen. There should be an option for you to see your Weekly Summary as well as change your move goal. Increase or decrease your goal number by tapping the – and + buttons and tap Update when you have decided.

The Activity app keeps track of your movement and gives a breakdown of the exercise you have done that day. On the home screen of the app, you will see the aforementioned three circles, but if you rotate the digital crown or swipe down on the display, you will see detailed information on when and what you are doing to reach your move goal.

While the Weekly Summary may prove somewhat informative, looking at the Activity app on your iPhone gives you many more data points to get a good idea of your performance for days, weeks, months, and even years. Go on to the Activity app and tap History, which is located in the lower left corner. You will see each calendar date coupled with the recurring three vibrant Activity circles/rings. Tap one of the dates to get the full breakdown of that day, just as you can on your Apple Watch, but only for a week's worth of activity.

The Activity app, if used, makes the Apple Watch feel much more like it is yours. It gives you personal information that can give you concrete data on how you live your life. Furthermore, there are achievements to be earned, so if you need some extra motivation, you can look on your iPhone for the various awards you can win by persevering towards your fitness goals.

2. The Workout app

Closely linked to the Activity app, the Workout app is a way to track whatever exercise you want to do swimming, cycling, running, power walking, and so on. After you select the tracker that suits the type of exercise you are doing, you can see, in general, the time you have spent working out, your heart rate, and distance traveled. You can always pause a workout by pressing the digital crown and the side button simultaneously and resume with the same command. The measurements gained from a recorded Workout will transfer over to the Activity app, giving you a wholistic idea of how many calories you have burned that day.

If you want to change the metric view or the system of measurement your workouts are being recorded in, you need to go to your Apple Watch app on your iPhone. Go to the My Watch tab and tap Workout and then Workout View. You will be able to select between a Multiple Metric View (the option of having up to five metrics shown on your screen while working out) or a Single Metric View (the option of having one metric displayed on the screen at one time; you can scroll the digital crown or swipe down to see the rest of the metrics). Also, prior to starting workout, you will be setting two goals for yourself: a calorie goal and a distance goal. For those who want their calorie goal in kilometers, force touch the screen and the option will pop up. The same can be done for your distance goal, but you will be choosing between yards/miles and meters/kilometers.

3. Make sure to enjoy Apple Music

This especially applies to those who have the Series 3 Cellular and bought a plan with a provider. Since you have the data, you can stream music for your daily life or workouts without needing to bring your phone along. Also, you need to use your monthly data anyways, so using it on streaming could be a good way to maximize your coverage.

But those with the GPS-only version of the Series 3 can still listen to music on the go, but they will need to bring their iPhone along. However, you can download your music to your Apple Watch so that you do not need cellular connectivity to listen to music. You will not have virtually limitless variety, but there is no extra charge involved. Depending on how much music you want to have on your watch, you might have to keep a watchful eye on your storage, though.

4. Download third-party apps

While Apple provides most of the basic apps you will need, it does not hurt to supplement your catalogue with third-party apps that can add a great deal of functionality to your Apple Watch.

i. Calcbot

Perhaps, to many people's understandable surprise, the Apple Watch does not come with a calculator app. Having the Calcbot app—just a basic calculator—makes paying exact tips much more convenient, for example. You will not need to take out your phone to make any calculation you might have to do in your daily life. The app is also free, which is always a plus.

ii. Evernote

Another surprising omission from Apple's stock apps, a note taking tool did not make the cut for the Apple Watch Series 3. Nevertheless, you can download Evernote for free so that you can take notes on the go. Notes are recorded through dictation.

iii. iTranslate

For those times when you are off adventuring in a country where English is not widely spoken or learned, the iTranslate app translates your sentences into the native tongue of the country you are visiting. Just dictate to the app and it will immediately output a translation for you. Gone are those awkward moments of gesturing and speaking slowly.

iv. *Sleep++*

With the prevalence of mattress commercials these days, proper sleep seems to be a great concern for most these days. Sleep++ monitors your sleep and gives you information on what you need to do to improve your nightly rest. This app could engender the healthy change you might need in your life.

v. *Uber*

Uber is premier ridesharing app, and you can get it on your Apple Watch Series 3. You will get all the information you would normally get through the phone version of the app (Driver ETA, car model, etc.).

5. **Remove the apps you do not want, even the stock ones**

Perhaps at one point in your life, you had an interest in the stock market, but now it does not bring you the enjoyment it once did. Your Apple Watch came with the Stocks app pre-installed, and you would rather use your storage for other apps. Apple has given users full authority on what apps they have on their watch, including the apps Apple designed for the watch. If you do not want it, you can delete it. Of course, you invariably have the option to download the Apple apps for free if you ever want to in the future.

Apple Watch 2018 Edition

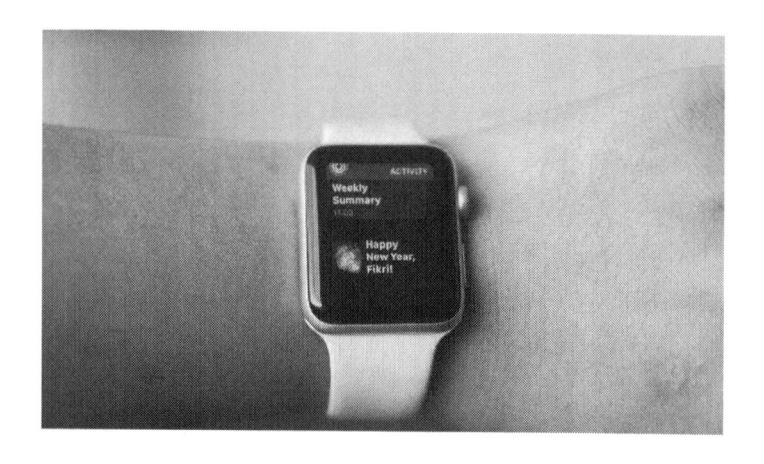

Part IV
Tips & Tricks

For lefties: If you are a left-handed person, you can change the watch orientation so the device suits you best. Simply go to the Apple Watch app on your iPhone and go to the General tab. Once there, click Watch Orientation.

Create multiple watch faces that you have customized: Creating multiple watch faces may not sound like something you want to do—you like a particular watch face and you are opposed to changing it. Sure, that could be the case, but having multiple watch faces allows you to quickly switch to a different design that best suits what you are doing. When you are exercising, you might want to select the Activity watch face with particular Complications. Later, you might be going to an upscale restaurant, so you want to go with the chronograph watch face. Creating multiple watch faces that you have customized to work with your tastes eliminates repeated alterations and time-wasting.

Forcing your Apple Watch to restart: Once in a while, devices tend to act up, suddenly slowing down or just refusing to function normally. Perhaps, your watch has frozen. In these cases, you can force restart your watch by pressing and holding the digital crown and side button simultaneously for ~10 seconds. You can cease holding when the Apple logo appears on the screen. Let it be known, though, force restarting your Apple Watch should be done as a last resort, per Apple. You should try to wait it out, instead. If nothing serious is wrong with the device, it should recover its optimal functionality soon enough.

Switching on power reserve: Perhaps, you are quickly running out of battery and you have left your phone at home. Turning on the power reserve mode on your Series 3 prolongs battery life so you will not have to worry about getting stranded somewhere without a functioning mobile device. This mode shuts off everything but your Series 3's ability to tell time. Supposedly, turning on power reserve mode extends battery life up to 72 hours. Thus, before your Series 3 reaches a critical battery state, you can turn on this mode so that when you need the juice to call someone later, your watch will have the requisite battery life to function. When your battery reaches a low percentage, your Apple Watch will automatically switch on power reserve; however, if you want to manually activate it, you need to go to the Control Center (swipe up from the watch face screen) and tap your battery reading. The option to turn on power reserve will be on that page.

Crafting your stock responses on Messages: For those times when you want to text something you often do—a "where are you?" or "Love you, X"—you can set up your personal stock responses to send through Messages.

Apple does provide a few pre-written messages, but if to someone you often text, such as your significant other, you can add a little personal flair to your pre-written responses. You can go about writing these stock responses on the Apple Watch app on your iPhone. Once the app has started, you need to go to the Messages setting and then tap Default Replies to craft your own stock responses.

Muting alerts with your palm: Apple provides an ingenious way to mute your alerts and notifications when you rest your palm over you Series 3. This means you do not have to go through the inconvenience of turning mute mode on and off. To activate this gesture, go to the My Watch app on your iPhone and tap Sounds & Haptics. Turn on the Cover to Mute. You will need to cover your Apple Watch for three seconds for it to register the mute command. You will know that the watch has been muted when it vibrates.

Taking photos with the Series 3: Lacking a camera to take photos, the Apple Watch Series 3 oddly comes with the Camera app pre-installed. This is for good reason, however. The Apple Watch Series 3 becomes a remote shutter trigger for your iPhone's camera. You simply need to open the Camera app on your Apple Watch and the same app will start on your paired iPhone. This way you can operate the camera while still being in the photo. So on those family trips when you want everyone to be present in the photo, the Apple Watch provides a solution.

Taking a screenshot: If, for whatever reason, you want to take a screenshot of what is currently on your Apple Watch display, you can press the digital crown and the side button simultaneously. The screenshot will be sent to your saved photographs.

Pinging your iPhone: Lost your iPhone? It happens to the best of us. But the Series 3 allows you to easily locate your iPhone by activating the Ping command from the watch's Control Center. Tap the icon with a phone and vibrations and your phone will vibrate and make a pinging noise. But, perhaps the ping is not enough. In this case, press the same icon, thus starting the LED flash on your phone and giving you a visual cue as to where your iPhone is.

Blocking water out from your Series 3: If you want to go for a swim or simply take a shower with your watch on, you can go to the Control Center and tap the icon with the water droplet on it. This will lock your watch casing, sealing it from exposure to water. This will also clear out the water from your Series 3's device. So in the case that water has gotten into the speaker, for example, tapping the water droplet will clear out any of that water blockage.

Setting your Series 3 a few minutes ahead: For those who want to make sure they are early rather than late to whatever they have scheduled, you can set your Apple Watch a few minutes ahead of the actual time so that you can remain on top of everything. To change the time on your Apple Watch, go to the Settings app, tap Time, and then just decide how much time you would like to add to the actual time. Remember: your notification, reminders, events, etc. will come in at that the actual time, not your personal time.

Unlocking your Apple computer(s) with the Apple Watch: If you own any Apple computer, the Apple Watch can be used to unlock your Mac without having to type in your password. First, you need to make sure both devices are on the same iCloud account. To set up the Series 3's unlock function, you need to go to System Preferences on your computer and then click on the General tab in Security & Privacy.

Set up Apple Pay: A veritably convenient app, Apple Pay gives you the liberty to go around without needing your credit and/or debit cards. Just go to the app and input your card information and you will be able to use the app to pay bills with your watch.

Checking your data usage: Maybe you are a workout fiend and have been going out on long runs every day of the month. You have been streaming music the whole time, and are worried about how much data you have been using. Oddly enough, you cannot check your data usage on the Apple Watch Series 3, so you will have to check it on your iPhone. To view your data usage, go to the My Watch app on your iPhone and then go to Mobile Data (it might show up as Cellular). Not only will you be able to see how much data you have used for the month, you will get a breakdown of how much data each of your apps are using. You can use these figures as a reference point for how you want to go about deploying your watch in the future.

Sending your location: If you are having trouble explaining your location to your friend, you can just share your location with your contacts. Using the Messages app, find the person you want to send your location information to and force touch the display. Three options will pop up: Reply; Details: and Send Location. Obviously, you need to tap Send Location and your current location, per GPS and GLONASS, will be immediately sent to that contact.

Enlarging text: If your sight is not the best, you have the option of increasing the text size in order for you to see the text on your Series 3 without having to squint. You need to go to the Settings app on your watch, tap General, and tap the Brightness & Text Size button. At this screen, select Text Size and rotate your digital crown to achieve the exact text size you desire.

Tips & Tricks

Tinker with your Apple Watch: The last tip is to simply play around with your Series 3 to see what you can get out of the different apps you already have on your watch or have downloaded. Tap around, force touch the display, swipe in all directions—just tinker with your watch. It does not hurt to know how to navigate your watch in the way that is most efficient for you. And who knows, you might discover some secret functions that will exponentially improve your efficacy.

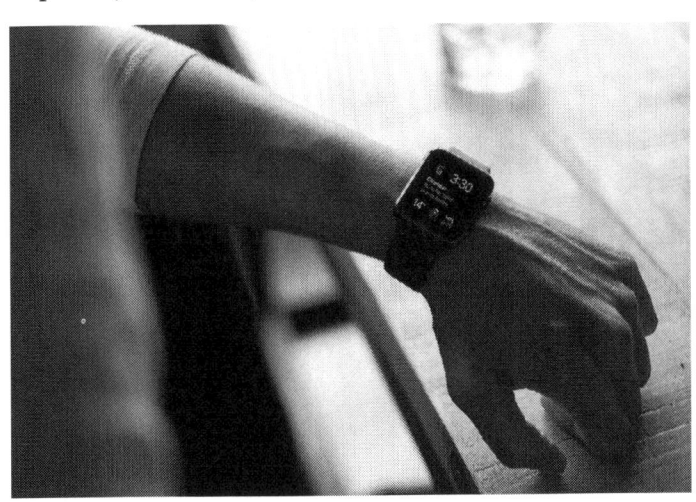

Conclusion

The possibilities to customize and personalize your Apple Watch Series 3 can prove daunting at times, but this guide has hopefully provided you with a comprehensive overview of everything you need to know about purchasing and using your timepiece. More than a traditional watch, where the functions and features are limited, the Apple Watch truly allows you to have an experience of your own that goes beyond the appearance and machinery of the watch.

In part I, this book covered all the available options for customizing the look of your Series 3. As with purchasing anything, it is always best to have researched what exactly goes into the product you desire. The jargon used to describe technological products especially sounds complicated and serves as good ad copy, however it is necessary to know what the tech does for you as the user. Perhaps, this book has informed you of the tech involved in the Apple Watch, while also supplying an exhaustive list of the cosmetic options available to you.

In part II, this book intended to furnish you with an in-depth tutorial on how to operate the Apple Watch Series 3. Navigating the watch can be difficult initially, but this book has all the information you need to figure out the basic operations and main apps of the watch. As you continue to use the watch, surely you will grow more and more comfortable with it; operating it will probably become second nature to you. Nevertheless, as you awkwardly fumble around with it in the early stages, you can always refer back to part II to get concise guidance on what you need to do to get your Apple Watch functioning the way you want it to.

In part III, this book went over one of the crowning features of the Apple Watch Series 3: the capacity to make the watch completely your own. Whether it be customizing your watch face design so that it works best for your life or setting your personal fitness goals, the Series 3 is crafted to be wholly yours. It seems injudicious to not personalize your watch so that it does exactly what you need/want it to do—that appears to be the whole point of a smartwatch! Ideally, this book encourages you to tinker around with your settings until you get the watch exactly how you want it.

In part IV, this book provided an exhaustive list of tips and tricks in using your Apple Watch Series 3. Following some of them will really give you the opportunity to maximize your usage of the watch. You will be patting yourself on the back when you lose your iPhone and can find it with the Ping command on your Apple Watch. Hopefully, you will not have misplaced both.

Conclusion

Ultimately, this book should have provided you with all the information you need to get the most out of your Apple Watch Series 3. No stone has been left unturned in the making and writing of this book.

APPLE WATCH

101 Helpful Tips and Secret Tricks

**Take Your Wearable Tech Game
to the Next Level**

Introduction

Congratulations on purchasing *Apple Watch: 101 Helpful Tips and Secret Tricks* and thank you for doing so.

The following chapters will discuss all things Apple Watch Series 3. If you are a tech-head or just a dedicated fan of the Apple Watch, then you probably already know that the Apple Watch Series 3 is the sleeker, faster, and more feature-packed iteration in the Apple Watch series. But, are you maximizing your use of this innovative device?

The huge leap forward in the Apple Watch Series 3 is its cellular capabilities that finally un-tethered users from total reliance on its iPhone pairing. The cellular feature brings with it a list of pros and cons, from the decision to incorporate an additional data plan cost to keep you running without total dependence on your iPhone, to the fact that cellular capability allows for fluid updates and notifications that seamlessly tie your iLife together. Automatic updates with Series 3 and crossover gear (think: AirPods, anyone?) create a personal relationship with the Apple Watch that supports the philosophy of better living through technology. Apple has clearly shown their hand in making a smartwatch that wants to make sure every aspect of your life is improved, managed, and entertained by tech. Nothing wrong with that!

Previous generations of Apple smartwatch made flipping through apps at the speed of life almost impossible and left users feeling that it was less the future they were wearing on their wrist, but a soon-to-be relic. Fortunately, Apple Watch Series 3 increased their confidence that their smartwatch is heading in the right direction. "It's fast, it's really fast," says CNET Senior Editor of Wearable Tech Scott Stein. "It's basically at the point where I wanted it to be three years ago" (Stein, 2018).

Don't fall behind! Dive into these 101 Helpful Tips and Secret Tricks to enrich your Apple Watch expertise and learn a captivating list of features to show off at parties. Nothing is a better conversation starter than, "Did you know my watch can do this?"

There are plenty of books on this subject on the market, thanks again for choosing this one! Every effort was made to ensure it is full of as much useful information as possible, please enjoy!

Chapter 1
Getting to Know Your Apple Watch Series 3

One of the best feelings in modern life is unpacking a shiny, new Apple product. If one thing has been consistent since the first iPod of the new millennium is that every white, beveled edge Apple design delivers that thrill of the future. The Apple Watch Series 3 is no different. The best way to start to hack this mini wonder of wearable tech is to make sure you have a firm understanding of its foundational components. If you have yet to make your wearable tech purchase, then you are in for a treat. If you are currently wearing your "squircle" faced watch, then reminiscence on that wonderful moment when you first unpacked, charged, and strapped it on.

This first chapter covers the basic terminology for the Apple Watch components and functions. Along the way, an introduction to the core decisions of setting up your Apple Watch is provided.

You are most likely already hip to the basics: the *side button* for power. Press and hold this button to turn on, and if already on, pressing and holding it will present button options to either turn off or contact Emergency SOS.

Tip & Trick #1*: Did you know that you can bypass the need to click "Emergency SOS" by holding down the side button for only 3 seconds?

A countdown will begin, and you will hear an alarm confirming the countdown and a slider will appear asking if you want to end the call or not. If you do not deny the call, then Apple Watch assumes that you are intending to automatically contact emergency services. While this makes it more likely for someone else's tight grip on your wrist (or your awkward napping position) to accidentally call 911, this intuitive feature makes a helpful SOS call in a worst-case-scenario during a crisis.

*For this feature to work, you must be within the range of your iPhone's Bluetooth connection, your wifi is connected, or your cellular is on and supported.

Tip & Trick #2: Well, wait. I don't want to accidentally call 911. How do I shut down the SOS feature?

There are pros and cons to having automatic 911 (or your country's emergency number) calling features. If your watch does happen to call 911 accidentally, do not panic. It is better to stay on the line and explain that there was a mistake then to hang up. Hang-ups on 911 have to be assumed by dispatchers as an emergency and police will show up to where the watch is located. This removes resources from real emergencies and probably adds an unexpected and unwanted element to your day.

To turn off this feature, you can go into your Watch app on your iPhone, select My Watch, and then choose General. Under this menu option, select Emergency SOS to turn the Hold to AutoCall slider off. If it is active, this slider is in green. You will still be able to hold down the side button for 3 seconds and have the option to call emergency services with a slider option, but this preferences setting will eliminate an accidental 3-second button push as an automatic conversation with 911 if not caught in time.

That little scroll wheel above the side button has an official name, and it's very regal. You ready? This click wheel is the *digital crown*. This king of the watch's mechanisms can be utilized in two ways: as a scroll wheel and as the *home button*. When pressing the digital crown at its center, you are accessing the home button or the equivalent of the central button on iPhones.

The Apple Watch *screen* is the digital display for all of the watches' communications. It likes to be off to help save your battery life. Your screen will be off when you are idle. To illuminate the screen, it's as simple as a flick of your wrist! Otherwise, you can tap the side button, home button, scroll the digital crown, or tap the screen itself.

Once awake, your Apple Watch is ready to go. To view all your apps, simply press the home button within the digital crown. A honeycomb-like colorful display of all your apps should appear. This arrangement of apps is called *Grid View*. If Grid View is your visual organizing system of choice, then all you need to do is touch and drag to navigate to the icon of your desired app. If you prefer a more traditional list, then please meet your next tip and trick:

Tip & Trick #3: Force Touch to Change Views.

Force Touch is when you touch the screen with more force than usual (like clicking and holding a traditional scroll pad on a laptop to left or right click). When you Force Touch on the Grid View screen, you will be presented with two options: Grid View and List View. Voila! List View achieved.

Within the more linear List View, you will be able to see the icon for each of your apps as well as their name. You can navigate through these by either scrolling the digital crown or by scrolling by touching the screen.

Next, meet your new favorite friend: *Complications*. What an odd name for such a useful tool. Complications are stored favorite apps that allow you to reload them without waiting for the whole app to reinvent itself upon every load. Complications hang out on your screen as an ever-present icon in one of three configurations: Circular Small, Utilitarian Small, or Utilitarian Large (these are smallest, small and square, and a long rectangular space, respectively). Complications are the widgets of the future. They allow you to keep your popular apps at hand and to keep these apps active with real-time updates.

Tip & Trick #4: Set up your Complications.

Do this easily by going into your Watch app on your iPhone. Select the My Watch tab at the bottom left-hand corner and select Complications. Here, you can add or remove the apps you would like featured as constant icons on your watch face. Once decided, you can customize which icon is shown for the Complication and also its placement. To do this, go to your watch face and tap to activate its editing mode. Tap on the visible Complications as this should highlight only one of the icons. You can now scroll using the Digital Crown to see what different icons can be displayed. Hold and drag the Complication to reposition its placement and therefore display according to its Circular Small, Utilitarian Small, or Utilitarian Large status. Each watch face will have a different division of real estate for where Complications can be held. This setup is worth playing around with for a while until you find what works for you. These buttons will be your most used apps and tools. A good question to ask while deciding Complications is, "What are my goals by using this smartwatch in my daily life?"

Tip & Trick #5: Use Complications wisely.

Utilitarian Large formatting allows Complications to provide limited, in-app data. This is useful for apps where you would like to have updates for on a regular basis such as: what your step count is, what the weather is like, how much money you are making on the stock market that day. If you religiously use your Apple devices for music, consider putting Now Playing as your Utilitarian Large Complication of choice. With this Complication, you can simply tap the Utilitarian Large area, and it will take you to the app player where you can control your music in an instant.

Dock. You know how, even with the best of intentions, you will open up one million tabs inside Google Chrome and then forget how you started with a mission to research intermittent fasting but wound up in a blog about tree farming in South Africa? Yeah, that's what your Dock is here for. Your Dock is where all your open and active apps hang out until you are ready to use them again or to remind you that you started an activity you forgot about in the middle of your Netflix binge. Your Dock is your patient best friend who lets you go on and on about your recent breakup and doesn't even bug you to change the subject! Access Dock by tapping the side button. You should see a portion of the app in your Dock with its most recent application status (how much money you have left in your Starbucks account, for example). Scroll through these with either the crown or your finger.

Tip & Trick #6: Customize your Dock for faster app load by using favorites.

Make sure you are staying focused or up-to-speed on which apps are important to you by customizing your Docks setting. Do this by going into your iPhone. Launch your Apple Watch App on your iPhone. Tap the My Watch tab in the lower left-hand corner. Select Dock from the main menu. You can either choose for your Dock to display Recent apps, or you can customize your Dock list. Add to your favorites list with abandon. Remember, those apps stored in your Dock will launch more quickly and be easier to find on the go (without sorting through your entire app list).

Tip & Trick #7: Don't waste time going from Dock back to List View or Grid View.

There is a Show All Apps button at the end of your Dock list. Use this. If what you are looking for isn't in your Dock, don't lose time (on a watch, no less!) backing up.

Tip & Trick #8: Make sure your screen looks like what you actually want it to.

There are two ways to do this, one is easy and one which requires a bit more patience. Let's go over the slower method first. Remember Force Touch? Go ahead and Force Touch once you are on the home screen. This should send the entire home screen into relief and signal that you can scroll through watch face options. You can either select a previous watch face design or add a New design. If you click New, you can scroll through preloaded designs provided by the Apple Gods. Click a new watch face and boom. Easy peasy. To customize the features of your watch face on your watch, Force Touch your desired watch face, and then scroll left and right to highlight the different elements of the design. You can then use the crown to scroll through all the permutations (colors, size, style). It takes time, but you can do it.

However, by changing your watch face on your Apple Watch, you will not get a preview of the new watch face with any established Complications. For this faster and more accessible method, head to your iPhone and open your Watch app. Select the Face Gallery tab at the bottom of the app screen. This is a nice View All spread of available faces (rather than one-by-one on the watch). Once here, you can then customize your watch face. You can change the color for some, and you can assign where your Complications will go. Once satisfied with your customizations, just click Add. Pretty nifty, huh?

Tip & Trick #9: Get rid of all those extra customized watch faces queuing up in one swipe.

Making a decision is hard, and having different options for your watch face may appeal to some, but it drives me nuts. For any Disney-fied or Modular watch face you are tired of coming across, go ahead, and press and swipe that face upwards. Apple is kind and asks if you are sure you want to Remove Buzz Lightyear. Click the Remove button and Poof! It is now deleted. You can also do this on iPhone within the My Faces section of the Watch app by clicking Edit and hitting the red Do Not Enter buttons by the undesired watch faces.

If you want to get extra-extra-customized, stay tuned for later in this guide.

Tip & Trick #10: Know your Control Center.

Just like your iPhone, your Apple Watch 3 has a Control Center. The functions here are the meat-and-potatoes of your smartwatch functions. Control how loud, connected, water resistant, and bothersome your device performs.

Get to it by swiping up on your watch home screen. In here you can:

- Check your battery life
- Connect to Bluetooth devices
- Mute your watch
- Control Airplane mode
- Toggle WiFi and Cellular connections
- Water Lock
- Silence Watch
- Enter Do Not Disturb
- Theatre Mode

The remaining components of your Apple Watch Series 3 include the microphone and speakers located stealthy on the left side of the device (of a left-wrist wearing user). The band that comes with your Apple Watch is obviously the band you will begin to despise within six months, but that is just the human aspect of falling in love and then living with your cool new piece of tech. Tips on dealing with this let down will pop up in Chapter 5.

Congratulations! You now have a solid beginning to understanding your Apple Watch. Now, let's look at the tips and tricks that will make your wearable tech useful, convenient, fast, and more fun.

Chapter 2
Maximizing Apple Watch Performance

One of the few pitfalls of the Apple Watch is its short battery life. Now, this is all relative, as the Fitbit can go for almost a full work week and then some while the Apple Watch Series is begging for a recharge after a day. However, the Apple Watch is the only smartwatch doing everything at once: fitness tracking, endless app options, messaging, GPS, and now, cellular. It kind of feels wrong to demand a robust battery for the sake of all these conveniences.

Regardless, you can go for the holy grail of running your Apple Watch with enough power saving tactics to maybe, maybe, go for two days without a recharge. It all comes down to your temperament. If making a nightly ritual out of recharging your devices is not a burden, then you can forgo most of these tips as dogmatic must-dos. Otherwise, use the tips and tricks of this chapter to manage the panic-inducing moments when you realize your watch battery is at its demise and you are scrambling to keep it alive just long enough to survive the long bus ride home.

Tip & Trick #11: Invest in the GPS + LTE Apple Watch Series 3, even if you won't end up using the cellular capabilities.

There is a good reason for this: storage. The Apple Watch Series 3 with cellular has a 16 GB capacity. This is *twice* the amount in the Apple Watch Series 3 without LTE. If you are on the fence about spending more money because you are uncertain if you like the idea of adding to your data plan, think about the leap as an investment in your performance. More memory means more apps, faster processing, and a lot more options to customize your Apple Watch experience. The cellular capability is a nice option to have, even if you do not see its use at the present.

Tip & Trick #12: Wake Screen on your schedule.

Go to the General menu, which is nested under your Settings app. You can customize your Wake Screen settings to better suit your preferences or your battery. To conserve energy, deselect any auto-wakes upon wrist flipping and audio app startups. It is a small change and may train you to tap your watch rather than bask in the automatic glory of a wrist flip, but it will give you more portable hours without a recharge.

Tip & Trick #13: Turn off your watch without waiting for the Wake Screen.

If you are impatient or paying extra attention to battery life, make it a habit to use your palm to press flatly against the screen. This is an extra quick way to make your device sleep.

Tip & Trick #14: Turn off your built-in heart rate monitor to spare battery life.

Apple Watch Series comes with a built-in heart rate monitor, which is a handy tool to get the real story on your fitness efforts. However, it uses too much battery. Go ahead and turn this function off by going to your Settings app, selecting the General menu, and scrolling down to Heart Rate Monitor. While it's noble to keep a tab on your ticker, this function is best left for intentional use during intentional workouts (and maybe not so much your trip to the grocery store). Don't worry, I assure you. Your heart is still beating even if this function is off.

Tip & Trick #15: Easy battery saver: Choose dark watch faces.

When selecting your watch face, consider that the more there is to the design, the more light and as well as power that design requires. Black and yellow colors will save the most battery life.

Tip & Trick #16: Power reserve will save your battery.

Make a habit of going to the Control Center (swipe up on your home screen) and checking in with your battery percentage (by tapping the battery icon). When you know you won't be maxing out your apps or anything watch-worthy for a while, tap on the battery icon and select Power Reserve. This is like Low Power mode on your iPhone. It will turn your smartwatch into only a watch (for the time being).

Tip & Trick #17: Save more power by changing preferences for Reduced Motion and Transparency.

Go to your iPhone Watch app, open the General menu, and select Accessibility. Turn off the Reduce Motion and

Reduce Transparency. This may take a little zing off of the watch experience, but you will benefit from not having to recharge every night.

Tip & Trick #18: Turn on Grayscale to save battery.

Under the iPhone Watch app, the General menu, and then Accessibility, turn on Grayscale to enable black and white shading on all Apple Watch features. Arguably, taking away the colors of Apple Watch destroys the sense of fun. However, this is a good survival tactic if you are not able to recharge your watch for the foreseeable future and are just trying to make it home.

Tip & Trick #19: Save power on your connected devices.

While in the Control Center, you can also select any connected devices and check in on their battery life. If you have AirPods connected by Bluetooth, you can then select the percentage display that correlates to their power level. You can now select Power Reserve for your device. Amazing!

Tip & Trick #20: Live in Airplane mode.

That airplane icon isn't just for when you are on a flight. Tapping Airplane Mode in the Control Center will turn off all radio transmitters from your watch. Think of Airplane Mode as the peaceful mode. Any connected devices, notifications, texts, interruptions from the outside world will turn off. This simple fix also temporarily spares your battery from background activities. Tap Airplane mode whenever you want to put a Do Not Disturb sign between yourself and the world. This can be an extra comfort when wearing such a connected device on your person, within your periphery, at all times.

Tip & Trick #21: Toggle from Cellular to Wireless or go off the grid.

In the Control Center, you will see two icons, one that looks like the traditional wifi icon and the other will look like a cellular tower icon (a pole that is radiating waves from a ball at its peak). *Be careful! The Cellular icon looks just like some traditional Airplane Modes on Apple Watch Series 3.*

When these are both on, your Apple Watch will seamlessly go back and forth between wireless and then switch into cellular when the wifi is lost in order to maintain an uninterrupted signal. Make sure your Apple Watch is using a connection that you approve of by setting your preference. Cellular or Wireless options are on when the button is highlighted. To turn off a connectivity option, simply press to remove the function.

Tip & Trick #22: Connect all your devices, even if you have no plan for all their uses yet.

Here is the one and only ringing endorsement in this guidebook for AirPods if, somehow, you have not already thrown them into your Apple Watch purchase. AirPods give you the freedom to use your Apple Watch Series 3 in the way it was intended: on cellular. You can take calls, listen to your music, and listen to secret voice memos while on-the-go. Go to the Control Center and select the Connect An Audio Device option (the triangle that radiates radio waves towards the bottom). Click this to connect AirPods, Bluetooth speakers, or any other audio accessory.

Tip & Trick #23: Write custom responses for messages.

When you receive a message notification, you are able to scroll down a list of pre-written responses. You can add to this list of options very easily for frequent responses you think you will need. Just go into your Watch app on the iPhone, go down to Messages, and then get into Default Replies. Scroll down to click Add Reply. This is where you insert your best, "I told you to never contact me again" or other inside jokes you need at the ready.

Tip & Trick #24: Slim down your app storage.

Unlike friendships, Apple Watch memory storage is not forever. Go to your iPhone Watch app and go to General.

Then, tap on Usage. This will give you a profile of how much storage each app is using on your Apple Watch. Delete as needed. Start with the bigger downloads first, and see if there are any that you can depart with without too many tears. This will help increase the speed and performance of your overall watch experience. Also, check in and see which apps may be overlapping in their functions. If you have both the Strava and Workout apps to help track your running, make the call if you can live without Strava and still meet your metric needs. Workout, as it is factory installed hardware, cannot be deleted.

Tip & Trick #25: Check in with Siri about your battery life.

You do not even need to pull up Control Center to check in on your battery status. Just go, "Hey Siri, what percentage is my battery?" Or some variation, and you will get a response in percentage.

Tip & Trick #26: Check in with Siri about the battery left on your iPhone.

As there is no way to access this information from Apple Watch via an app or Control Center, it is a pretty great thing to be able to ask Siri, "Hey Siri, how much battery is left on my iPhone?" And get a percentage response even if you are miles away from your phone.

Chapter 3
Navigation & Notifications

The tips and tricks presented in this chapter are imperative to your stress-free experience of controlling your Apple Watch. As usual with Apple products, there is always a clunky way to perform an action, and then the intuitive (although often secret) fluid way to perform a function. This chapter highlights these fast-as-you-can options.

An almost existential question is also how to manage your notifications. Your Apple Watch can be your home base for reviewing these, or you may choose to refer to your iPhone to deal with the onslaught of communication and reminders. The good news is that you can determine how much you want to be bothered (I'm sorry, reminded) and by what.

Take care to spend a lot of time with these tips to build a strong navigational foundation. It will save you scads of time down the road when you would have to unlearn a built-in habit to get to the simpler solution. It is recommended to read each tip and then physically perform the task to make sure your muscles build the memory.

Tip & Trick #27: What is that red dot?

No, it's not a bindi. A red dot at the top of your watch face means that you have notifications. Feel popular and then see Tip #39 to learn how to delete them all at once. You can pull down from this red dot to view your line up.

Tip & Trick #28: Silence incoming calls quickly.

When a call is coming into your smartwatch, you do not even have to aim to hit the call reject or accept buttons to take action. You can just place your palm, lightly but firmly, over the watch face. This will silence the call automatically. The call will still continue, and you can then choose to take action, but the ringtone will be muted.

Tip & Trick #29: Flip your view between an open app and the most recently used app.

A handy trick is to double click the home button within the digital crown, and this will flip the view back to your most recent app. Double click again and you'll get back to your current app.

Tip & Trick #30: Zoom when you need to.

Skip going to your iPhone to adjust text size and use the Zoom feature on a case-by-case basis. Get into your Settings, then under General, and then under Accessibility, you'll find the Zoom status. Click this to turn it on, and now you can activate Zoom by tapping two fingers at once on the screen. This will Zoom the image, and you can scroll around by touching two fingers and dragging the view.

Tip & Trick #31: Force reset when Apple Watch freezes.

Just like us, smartwatches have bad days. If your Apple Watch is struggling and is timing out, go ahead and hold down the home button within the digital crown and the side button at the same time. This will force your Apple Watch to restart and force a hard reset.

Tip & Trick #32: Adjust Haptic strength.

Make sure you are comfortable with the Haptic strength of your notifications. Haptics are the light taps or vibrations that alert you, instead of sound, to a notification. Go to Settings, then General menu, and then tap Sounds & Haptics. There will be a slider bar to adjust the strength under the Haptic field.

Tip & Trick #33: Choose what watch face you return to.

By default, after your watch has been asleep, it will wake up to the home screen of the digital clock. You can change this by going into your iPhone app and selecting General settings. Here, scroll down and select "Activate on Wrist Raise" to change the default option from Show Watch Face to Show Previous Activity. This will keep your watch work more in flow with where you left off.

Tip & Trick #34: Boost your Haptic strength.

If the above adjustment is not enough, you can go to your iPhone watch app and select Sounds and Haptics. Enable Prominent Haptic slider at the bottom of the menu. This will maximize your physical alerts.

Tip & Trick #35: Force Close an app without a hard reset of the entire Apple Watch.

On the rare occasion an app times out or stalls, you can force-close the app without restarting the watch. Press and hold the side button until you see the power screen options pop up with two sliders: Power Off or Power Reserve. Do not choose either and just go ahead and hold down the side button again. This will force close the current app and take you back to either your List View or Grid View.

Tip & Trick #36: Press and hold down the Digital Crown to get to your home screen.

Quick, easy, done.

Tip & Trick #37: Get in touch with your notifications.

Spare yourself from rummaging around elsewhere and go to the home screen. Pull down from the top to see your notifications. You can scroll through this one-by-one.

Tip & Trick #38: Delete notifications one by one.

While scrolling through your notifications, when you come across one that you'd like to either ignore or just not review again, swipe on the alert from right to left. A "Close" option will pop up to confirm the delete and press the X button to say yes. It's just like Tinder: swipe left to forget about it.

Tip & Trick #39: Clear all notifications at once.

Maybe you are blowing up one day and need a break, or maybe it is just the normal course of having too many WhatsApp, Messenger, Facebook, Twitter, Instagram, and Email alerts begging for your attention. Practice serenity now by closing all notifications at once. Do this by going to your notification screen by pulling down from above on your home screen. Then, Force Touch anywhere on the screen. A "Clear All" option will appear and press the X to confirm.

Tip & Trick #40: Prevent notifications from popping up in the first place.

For this, just go into your iPhone Watch app and tap on Notifications in the main menu. Enable the Notification Privacy. This will prevent notifications from popping up on your smartwatch. This may be a good tactic to take overall since you'll be greeted with notifications once back on your phone. You can keep your Apple Watch as a special "me time" timepiece.

Tip & Trick #41: Go nuclear.

Want to start your life over? Well, the life of your Apple Watch, that is. Turn back time by going to Settings, then select General menu, and then find that Reset button at the bottom. Warning: This will reset all, and I mean all, of your Apple Watch settings. But sometimes, a clean start is the best way to turn down the noise in your life.

Tip & Trick #42: Decide how you want to be bothered.

Notifications. So easy to love, so easy to hate. Go to your Settings app and select Sounds & Haptics. Sounds are self-explanatory, but Haptics is a fun change of pace. They are physical alerts in place of sound notifications (a light tap on your wrist).

Tip & Trick #43: Make friends with Siri and set her up.

To activate Siri, just tap the home button within the digital crown. Now say, "Hey Siri…" and this will wake her up. A useful Apple Watch Siri command is "Hey Siri, Launch Settings [or any other app name]…" Saves you time from scrolling and swiping through your grid view.

Tip & Trick #44: Tell Siri to sleep if you accidentally wake her up.

If you "Hey Siri…" and either change your mind or have become self-conscious talking to your watch, just say "nevermind" to cancel your Siri command. She won't mind.

Tip & Trick #45: Hand Off your watch app to your iPhone.

Work seamlessly by picking up where you left off on your watch. All you have to do is start your iPhone and notice the icon at the lower left-hand corner. This should be an icon of the active app on your watch. Pull this icon up to access your unlocked screen. Enter your code or touch ID, then voila! Your open watch app is now in its exact same place on your iPhone.

Tip & Trick #46: Save steps by using Quick Lock to better navigate apps.

If you want to go out of an app and back to a centered Grid View, you can tap the home button out, then tap again and then once more to re-center. Or, you can plant your palm over the watch face to activate Quick Lock. This automatically closes the watch. Then, flip your wrist to wake Apple Watch back up. Now, tap the home button and poof, you are back to a centered Grid View.

Tip & Trick #47: Send messages fluidly with auto send.

Once you establish your reply, either default or a voice memo, you can just tap anywhere on the screen to confirm a send. You do not have to aim your finger at the miniature "Send" hyperlink text.

Tip & Trick #48: Know when people messaged you.

Within the Messages app, just hold and slide the screen to the left in order to see the timestamps of each message. This helps you determine if you should respond ASAP or send a friendly reminder that you asked your dad three days ago if he wanted to go for a hike.

Tip & Trick #49: Mirror your Do Not Disturb settings with your iPhone.

The Do Not Disturb function is a relief for those who need a notification break on the daily. If you go to your iPhone Watch App and select Do Not Disturb, you will see an option to Mirror iPhone. Enable this slider so that whenever your iPhone is scheduled for Do Not Disturb mode, your Apple Watch will be too. This saves you from repeating your efforts within the Apple Watch Settings menu.

Chapter 4
Hack Your Life: How to Utilize Apple Watch Series 3 to Improve Time Management, Fitness, and Self-improvement

The long game Apple is running is a bid on your full attention regarding all self-help projects. It is reasonable to say they are succeeding. Technological advances mean nothing if they cannot connect with the human experience. On one hand, technology is at a saturation point where there is nothing vital needed. You can now talk to someone instantly, by voice, video, or text. You can map directions, leave reviews, book reservations, buy almost anything, make travel plans, watch a movie, and plot your creative goals *all on your watch*. Further advancements feel indulgent, almost like they are gilding the lily.

This is where the Apple ecosystem excels. The vital space still in need of innovation is the eternal quest for self-improvement. How can you utilize your wearable tech to help you enrich your life? How can you interface with Apple Watch to better structure your day? These are not just conveniences but realized self-determined goals. Think of your Apple Watch as the bridge between your goals and accountability. The quicker you can reframe your relationship to the smartwatch as one that is part personal coach, part therapist, part personal assistant, and part motivational speaker, the richer your rewards will be. Technology is just a tool, yes. But, in the hands of Apple, technology becomes a personal revolution capable of changing your life.

Think small (as small as an Apple Watch app!) and take each tip one step at a time. These small steps and attention to detail will add up to form the bigger and brighter picture of a transformed you.

Tip & Trick #50: Be on time.

What is the real point of having a luxury watch if you are going to be late? Oh right, it is super cool. Well, let's start with one of the virtues: Being on time. For most of us, it is a struggle. Go to Settings (this will be in your selected app display in either Grid View or List View). Tap the Time option. Here, you can add 5, or 10, or 30 minutes in the classic attempt to beat the clock. Go ahead and do it. Your mileage (and time savings) may vary.

Tip & Trick #51: Know the weather to better plan your day by setting the correct city.

You can change your location for the Weather app by going into the iPhone Watch app, hitting My Watch, selecting Weather, and defining your current location. Adjust this for the city you are traveling to so you can pack better.

Tip & Trick #52: Use Siri to set a timer.

"Hey, Siri, set a time for 45 minutes." You would be surprised, but this is the #1 app that smartwatch clad users go to every week. Maybe it makes some sense to keep track of time on a watch, but the usefulness of having a countdown when it comes to cooking, napping, completing chores, setting a work goal, setting a shopping time limit, keeping track of your reading and studying, or just reminding you how much time you have to diffuse a bomb cannot be overstated. Life happens in real time so get hip to how to make the most of it by using this favorite Siri command.

Tip & Trick #53: Maximize the Weather app to get all the information.

Once open, the Weather app will display the weather in icon format. Tap the watch face, and it will rotate through exact temperatures in Celsius and Fahrenheit, then again for a likelihood of rain. If you Force Touch, you can get a button view of these options.

Tip & Trick #54: Find your f#!$%*g iPhone!

Go to the Control Center. See that phone icon that has waves radiating from it? That is your new best friend. Tap the icon because that is the Pinging iPhone button. Your iPhone, wherever she is, will then audibly ping. Hold down this icon to emit bright flashes of light from your iPhone to relocate it after you accidentally let it fall into a deep, dark crevasse.

Tip & Trick #55: Get your Flashlight on.

Go to the Control Center and tap the Flashlight icon. The screen goes white but dim. Not too impressive, eh? Flip the watch away from you, Apple Watch knows, and the illumination will increase. A handy little tip for when you are heading to the bathroom at 3 AM and do not want to wake the house.

Tip & Trick #56: Get a customized Flashlight on.

Wait, there's more? Of course. Swipe left or right once in Flashlight to start a strobe function, or even to get a red light (easier on the eyes in the dark). For those fighting crime, use the former to deter your enemies. For those solving mysteries, use the latter to keep your sleuthing low-key.

Tip & Trick #57: Do Not Disturb.

Get rid of all notifications or anything else that may disrupt your 14-hour writing marathon (you are working on your novel, right?). Click the moon icon in Control Center. Do Not Disturb will be set for the schedule as it is determined in your iPhone app. If you want to change or set a usual standard of 12:00 AM to 8:00 AM, do this in your iPhone now. Do Not Disturb and therefore, chill.

Tip & Trick #58: Forget the Apple Calculator App and go for something that makes sense.

Having a mathematician on your wrist will always be useful. Go ahead and do not waste your time with the awkward factory calculator app that comes with Apple Watch Series 3. DialCalc is an ingenious solution that works with the limitations of the smartwatch UX. The clever app makes both numbers and functions live on a dial that you can rotate through to set up your equations.

Tip & Trick #59: Avoid disappointment from browsing the regular App Store.

Wearable technology is still new and somewhat of a programmer's nightmare in making long-standing apps responsive in its microform. Make sure to only go on the hunt for watch apps from the App Store link from within the Watch app on your iPhone. This specialized version of the App Store only displays apps that are compatible with the Apple Watch Series.

Tip & Trick #60: Theatre Mode to be a good citizen.

When you go and watch a movie or your child's school play, be kind and select Theatre Mode in the Control Center. These are the drama mask icons. In this mode, Apple Watch will be on silent mode, and its screen will not wake up unless you tap or press a button.

Tip & Trick #61: Swim like a pro.

Now, this is cool. If you are like many of us humans and get the most motivated to work out when you track your progress and workouts with precise metrics, then Apple Watch Series 3 will get you gunning to jump in the pool. Go to the Control Center and click that water drop icon. This is Water Lock. It will turn off any watch response to taps or accidental button hits while swimming. To turn off Water Lock, you will have to turn the Digital Crown. When you do this, it turns off Water Lock mode and *ejects any water that may have filled the speakers during your workout.*

As always, when you add water with technology, there are some inherent risks. Water resistance can and will deteriorate over time. Utilizing Water Lock will help mitigate this wear and tear. Apple Watch Series 3 (and Series 2) is water resistant (not waterproof) with a water-resistance rating of 50 meters under ISO standard. This means that you can take your Apple Watch Series 3 for a shallow swim, a splash in the pool, and casual water activities. Any serious scuba diving (or deeper than a top-surface butterfly or backstroke) should not be attempted. Also, if you wind up in a body of saltwater, extra care should take place afterward. Wipe your smartwatch with fresh water and use a linen cloth to dry.

Tip & Trick #62: Water Lock like a pro.

Go ahead and repeat Water Lock mode even after getting out of the pool. Remember that ejecting water function from your speakers? Spare yourself extra dry time and repeat until you hear a free and clear airway after several expels.

Tip & Trick #63: Hike and bike like a pro.

One of the really cool new features of the Apple Watch Series 3 is the Barometer. This measures changes in altitude. This will benefit bicyclists and hikers as they can now include metrics about their elevation gains and descends accurately from just wearing their watch. Just access your Workout app or head to the App store (remember: within your iPhone Watch app menu) to browse elevation tracking apps.

Tip & Trick #64: Workout with precision.

Go to the General menu, under the Settings app, and get into the nitty-gritty of how your workout tools are performing. For the most part, Apple Watch Series 3 will default to auto-detect Bluetooth gym equipment and to precisely track your runs (or well-intentioned jogs!) by only tracking while you are actually moving. There are workarounds by deselecting these options and using your workout apps. If you are worried about saving battery life, then opt for turning off the heart rate monitoring that is a built-in feature of Apple Watch Series 3 and will start tracking whenever your watch detects not just running but walking. By turning off the heart-rate monitor, you bought yourself the luxury of leaving auto-walk and auto-run detect functions on.

Tip & Trick #65: Workout App is your friend in fitness, and you can add activities.

This app comes standard with Apple Watch, and it is one not to be ignored. Once you launch Workout from your App view, you can select various cardio activities you are about to participate in, and the app will track your caloric burn, effort, and progress towards goals. If you have an activity that you do not see in the selection, such as weightlifting, do not fear. You can select Other and rename the activity. This will now be saved as an option in the future.

Tip & Trick #66: Make sure to integrate the Activity App between your iPhone and Apple Watch.

Your fitness progress report is going to show up in your Activity App, which is readily available on your iPhone. But make sure, if you are keen on using Apple Watch to improve your health, to select the Activity App as one of your Complications. The little bullseye icon will keep your metrics fresh within the mind, and the 30-minute exercise goal limit (that cannot be changed) in the app makes sure you maintain a healthy and reasonable daily goal.

Tip & Trick #67: Beware of the Stand ring in the Activity App.

The innermost circle in the Activity app is supposed to track your standing time during the day. Unfortunately, Apple Watch Series 3 is most likely to count your sit time as standing time. Why does this matter? It may not to you, but for those paying attention to their daily output, it can be a bit of a bummer to get credit for calories burned that did not in fact happen.

Tip & Trick #68: Set up Wallet to utilize Apple Pay.

I know, I know. The world is ending, and the banks know everything about us. And yet, there is nothing more convenient than not having to remember or lug out your credit card every time you have to make a purchase. Setting up Apple Pay is easy to do. You just have to add an eligible credit, debit, or prepaid card to your Apple Watch. Open the Watch app on your iPhone. Go to the My Watch tab in the bottom left-hand corner. Select Wallet & Apple Pay and follow the instructions for entering your card information. Your bank will be asked to verify if the card is eligible for Apple Pay and may require further verification. Once all is on the up-and-up, you are ready to use your watch to purchase goods and services in stores, online, within messages, in apps, and on transit. The possibilities! Basically, anywhere you can see one of these symbols the Apple Pay symbol or Tap to Pay symbol.

Tip & Trick #69: Get to your payment card quickly with Wallet.

Avoid going through the hassle of finding the Wallet app, especially after you just ordered your medium latte with almond milk and there is a line of tired, grouchy customers waiting behind you. Double click the side button (not the home button) and your default payment card should appear. Hold this near the contactless reader on the payment machine. Wait until you feel a gentle Haptic (tap) on your wrist confirming the payment went through. Presto!

Depending on the machine, it may ask you to select debit or credit for processing your smartwatch transaction. Go ahead and select credit. Debit transactions may require entering your PIN as you would with a normal payment method.

Tip & Trick #70: Pay with a different card than your default selection.

Very easy: follow the instructions above. Double tap the side button and then swipe right or left to browse through the payment cards you have on file through your iPhone.

Tip & Trick #71: Save yourself time with online purchases and checkouts.

Make sure your billing address details are stored in your iPhone Apple Pay information. This way, while checking out and buying that sweet summer hammock on your smartwatch, all you will have to do is click "Buy With Apple Pay" and avoid the slow work of confirming where your bills go to.

Tip & Trick #72: Set up Calendar in a way that makes sense to your brain.

Some people are more visual learners, and some people need information in the most linear way possible. Open your Calendar App and click and hold on the screen to adjust to your needs. The options you have are List View, Day view, and Today. If you click Today at the top of the app, it will link you back to a monthly calendar view and allow you to tap into any day of the week, month, or year.

Tip & Trick #73: Let friends and family know where you are by quickly sending location information.

Within Messages, while you are chatting away with a buddy, you can easily share your location status by Force Touching the watch face. This will bring up three options, one of which is "Location." Tap this, and Apple Watch will let your buddy know which Starbucks you are currently waiting for them and how it was not the one further down the street.

Tip & Trick #74: Stay in your zone even while playing music.

When you are using the Music app to play tunes, anytime you awaken your watch, the watch face will automatically display your Now Playing screen. This may be your cup of tea, but if you regularly let a playlist go and get on with your life, you can go to Settings, General, and then Wake Screen to adjust this preference. Turn off the Auto-Launch Audio Apps option so that you can start the music and then continue on with normal app use with no interruptions.

Chapter 5
Customization: How to Make Apple Watch Reflect Your Style and Personality

It is just a fact that you will use your Apple Watch more if it fits your style and personality. The worst feeling is wearing the somewhat bulky technical marvel and not feeling like it is a part of your lifestyle. This chapter cracks open the hidden options for customizing your watch display and common pitfalls to avoid when purchasing.

It is also important to set your security preferences so your watch does not seem like a stranger to you. It's a humble user. You can utilize the intuitive security features of Apple Watch to make sure access is a breeze.

Are you a Lefty suffering in a Right Hander's world? Do not fret. Apple Watch also provides the option to reverse wrist-wearing orientation so you, the more creative of dominant hands, do not feel left out.

Best practices also recommend culling your app list on occasion to make sure they are serving both you and your storage needs. Read on to start making your Apple Watch feel like home.

Tip & Trick #75: Customize your watch face with your own photos and downloads.

If you have watchOS 4 or iOS 11, you can utilize photos on your iPhone as watch face design options. Start on your iPhone and use the Share Sheet. Get to your desired image and press the Share button. Then, scroll through and choose the Create Watch Face button. You will have two options, either a screen-filling Photos Watch Face or Kaleidoscope Watch Face. You can then customize the watch face as you did in Chapter 1. Lucky you on making the upgrade! Apple rewards you with more ways to be your unique self (and punish those hanging out still in iOS 10).

You can also change the watch face to a personal photo from the watch itself. Go ahead and tap the watch face to get into the editor, scroll right until you see New, tap the Add button, and then keep scrolling until the Preset options are run through, and you will start to see the photos available on your iPhone (as long as you are within Bluetooth range of your phone). It is a beautiful thing when you can make your own face, the face of time.

Tip & Trick #76: Third-party Complications.

While the starter set of Complications are fine and dandy, did you know that you can add in Complications from third-party apps? The key is to get into your iPhone Watch app. From here, click Complications at the top of the screen and a list of already downloaded apps that are available as Complications will be displayed. Choose wisely! There is only so much Complication real estate on your watch face.

Tip & Trick #77: Change the orientation of your screen to match with which wrist you wear your Apple Watch on.

Go to the General menu. General is nested under Settings (which is one of your Apps). Under the menu, tap Orientation. You can flip the function of the Digital Crown here, too, to accommodate a wrist flip.

Tip & Trick #78: Passcode perfection.

Go to the Settings app, get into the General menu, and select Passcode. You can then determine some pretty handy customizations. If you turn Wrist Detection on, this means your Apple Watch will notice when you are not wearing your device and automatically lock your watch. Unlock With iPhone is another handy setting to keep on. This setting means that anytime you unlock your iPhone, it will also unlock your Apple Watch. This will save you the trouble of entering your passcode upon every smartwatch access point.

Tip & Trick #79: Text you can actually read.

Access your Watch app on iPhone and select Brightness & Text Size. This might take some trial and error between selecting a preference and then giving it a test run to see if you like its effects. Know that adjusting via iPhone is the only way to manipulate these core functions.

Tip & Trick #80: Buy the other watch bands. Yeah, I said it.

This is more of a morale booster than secret, coveted tip. If you are debating whether it is worth over the sixty dollar splurge on a different band, or maybe the same band or just a different color, go for it. What you are actually investing in is the usefulness and convenience of a larger expense. The idea is to make sure this piece of technology improves your life. If you dare not wear your model because it does not look appropriate for an event, or does not match your outfit for the day, then why even has it in the first place? Of course, Amazon offers deep discounts on bands from overseas, but you can try to order these at your own risk.

Tip & Trick #81: Do not purchase the Ceramic Back Apple Watch Series 3 and pair it with a Stainless Steel band.

One of the most heartbreaking moments in owning a new piece of tech is the first incidence of damage. Whether it's a ding, a scratch, or a crack, it's a feeling of loss that is hard to not blame yourself for. Be warned, though. The Ceramic Back Apple Watch Series 3, which is only available on the Series 3 without cellular capabilities, is prone to scratching from metallic surfaces. It would go to reason then that placing a stainless steel, svelte-looking band next to this porous surface will not end well.

Tip & Trick #82: Arrange apps in the order you want.

Honestly, this technique is easier to edit while in your iPhone app, but you can do this in the watch. Just tap lightly (not a Force Touch) on your Grid View display. You will then recognize the shaky, alive status of all the apps just waiting for your instructions. Drag and drop your apps to arrange in the pattern of your choosing. Go wild and organize by a color code scheme for a peaceful look.

Tip & Trick #83: Delete apps you no longer want (from your Apple Watch only).

As always, you can only delete third-party applications and cannot delete the factory preset apps. Just tap lightly on your App view and activate the Shaky app-mode and you will see the small little Xs at their corners. Precisely tap these Xs to delete an app. The nice part is, this will only delete the app on your watch and not on your iPhone. You will receive a confirmation screen, so do not worry about the likely event that your normal-sized finger will accidentally hit the incorrect minute app.

Tip & Trick #84: Line 'em up!

You can arrange your app icons in Grid View in a single file line. It may seem impossible, but a dedicated user can do it. Go into your iPhone Watch app, and get to the app Grid View settings menu. Go ahead and drag each icon, one by one, to latch onto the last outlier. It's soothing. It's like knitting, but for your eyes.

Chapter 6
Have More Fun: Personal Communication & Entertainment On-The-Go

It is a safe bet to make sure that you purchased your Apple Watch Series 3 not just to help streamline your life but to have a little fun. There are some smart preliminary steps you can take now to make sure that when you are ready to access your entertainment apps, they are ready to perform without a hitch. This includes making sure you have the right gear.

A necessary step to maximizing your Apple Watch Series 3 experience is to invest further into the Apple ecosystem with a pair of AirPods (image below). Now, yes, this is exactly what Apple wants you to do. And, yes, it feels criminal that Apple Watch will not un-tether itself from Apple gear. Just like an amusement park, once you are on Apple's premises, you are invested in the full experience and cannot compare prices with competitors or with their specs. The happy news is that AirPods are worth the $159 (£159) investment. These little guys will keep you seamlessly engaged with your Apple Watch and iPhone, let alone any other Bluetooth gear you would like to connect to your support grid.

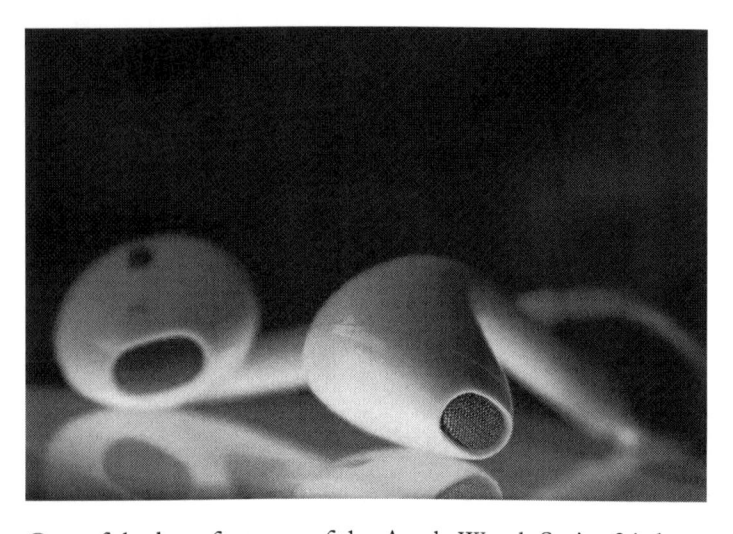

One of the best features of the Apple Watch Series 3 is how it can keep you connected with its eellular capabilities even away from your iPhone. This chapter covers the best practices for communicating with your friends, making Messaging less of a headache, and unlocking the surprise features that make Apple Watch 3 the most playful iteration of its series.

Tip & Trick #85: Field incoming calls with more options than just Accept and Reject.

An incoming phone call can induce panic in some and annoyance in others. If you are one of the few still partial to the lost art of phone conversation, then this is good for you. Otherwise, know that when an incoming call is being received, you can pull up from the bottom of the screen to display two additional options, Send a Message or Answer on iPhone.

Tip & Trick #86: Group your friends together for faster group communication.

Spend some time and effort within the iPhone app under the Friends menu option. The order you place your frequent contacts and the blank spaces that appear under this option will be reflected visually within your watch app.

Tip & Trick #87: Use Friends view to know which of your contacts also have Apple Watch.

Go to the Friends app and scroll through your dial of contacts. If you tap their profile picture, this will pull up options to message or call, but if there is a hand icon at the center bottom of the screen, this means your friend is also living the Apple Watch life.

Tip & Trick #88: Watch face Easter Eggs.

An Easter Egg is a gaming term for a hidden event or fun surprise within a game. In here, if you double tap your watch faces, an animation will occur, specific to that design. Tap the world image watch face and get a tour of the solar system!

Tip & Trick #89: Easter Egg Watch Faces.

Spend time with the Earth and Sun watch faces. If you zoom in or out on these watch faces, they seamlessly morph from the celestial body into the icon for your home screen app. Also, if you tap the Earth watch face into its Solar System layout, try double tapping the Solar System view to have the planets align with their names. It is a pretty cool feeling to have all nine planets (we'll still include Pluto, the dwarf planet) all lined up for you on your wrist.

Tip & Trick #90: Start by playing your music from your watch by putting your music on your watch.

This time investment pays off three-fold in terms of convenience. Go ahead and open the Watch app on your iPhone, select Music, and then select which songs you would like to load on your watch. If you are mainly using your Apple Watch for music listening purposes, load everything. If you are only using your Apple Watch for workouts, then create some gym-engineered sweat song playlists to upload in order to save space. Select upload and wait for the magic to happen. Now, your songs will go with you wherever you go.

Tip & Trick #91: Access more music controls.

Inside the Music app, Force Touch to view the controls for Shuffle, Repeat, Source, and Air Play. If connected to wireless or Bluetooth near your iPhone, you can change the speakers that are playing your music from your AirPods to your iPhone speakers. This is true for any additional Bluetooth speakers you may connect.

Tip & Trick #92: Take pictures like a pro.

Your Apple Watch can assist you in using your iPhone camera better. Open the Apple Watch Camera app and you will initially get a view of whatever your iPhone camera is seeing. To view yourself through your Apple Watch, change to the front view camera on your iPhone and position the iPhone towards you. The handy detail is that the Apple Watch offers a timer so you can take arranged photos without needing to contact your iPhone. You can also just hit the snap circle on your Apple Watch and this will trigger the iPhone camera to take your best selfie. Use this function to take better fur baby photos as well! If you have a wriggly animal, you can pick them up and fool them into believing you are just hanging out for a snuggle fest, when in actuality you have propped your iPhone up and were only waiting for the best moment on Fluffy's face to snap a photo from your smartwatch.

Tip & Trick #93: Skip using the in-app button to snap pictures.

That little button is small and cozy right next to the 3-second delay. Skip this exercise in precision and use the side button to snap a photo on your iPhone.

Tip & Trick #94: Make Mickey or Minnie Mouse tell you the time.

Go to Settings and under the General menu, find Sounds & Haptics. Scroll down and make sure Tap to Speak Time is on. Now, when you tap your home screen digital clock, guess who tells you what time it is on the dot? Now, if they only do something freaky and get a Steve Jobs watch face going…

Tip & Trick #95: Take screenshots!

Yes, so very simple and satisfying to do. First, make sure the function is enabled in your iPhone Watch app by going to the General under Settings and turning on the Enable Screenshots slider. Just press the digital crown and side button at the same time on your Apple Watch, and snap! The screenshot will be shared with your iPhone.

Tip & Trick #96: Scroll through Messages quickly.

It can be a pain to use the digital crown to wind through a long conversation. Within the Messages app, instead of scrolling, tap the top of the app field where your conversation mate's name appears. This will automatically rewind back to the top of your conversation.

Tip & Trick #97: Really tell Siri to go away.

If you are not in the mood, you can dismiss Siri with the voice commands, "Piss off!" or "Go away!" She'll buzz off accordingly.

Tip & Trick #98: Customize the color of your Emoji responses.

In Messages, you can reply with Emojis as an option. Once this option is selected, you will see enlarged versions of common emojis you can swipe through. If you Force Touch on these large Emojis, it will change their color. Keep Force Touching until you land on the perfect shade of blue for your heart.

Tip & Trick #99: Get to your Emoji history quickly.

If you are like most users, your Emoji palette has a favorite hit list. In Messages, reply to a chat with the Emoji option. Then, swipe left until you reach the far right screen. This will be a matrix of your most recent Emoji history to pull from. Quickfire those manicured nails and salsa dancing girl!

Tip & Trick #100: Set your preference for audio responses within Messages to streamline your replies.

The dictation method of sending a response text can be a bit intimidating to the uninitiated, but the technology here is pretty outstanding. However, when using an audio response (vs. a default reply), Messages will ask you after your audio recording if you want to send a dictation of the transcript (text) or the voice memo. You can set your preferences within the iPhone Watch app so that Messages will always default to one method or the other. Just head to the Watch app, select Messages, and tap Audio Messages. There are three options in here. Select Always Audio for voice memos, Always Dictation for text, or Dictation or Audio, so that Messages always let's you choose.

Tip & Trick #101: Use Scribble app to type out replies or anywhere you need notes.

Scribble is a fun app that lets you finger-draw a letter that it will then convert into a digital type. The extra hack here is to use the digital crown to scroll through possible word complete options after several letters. So, Scribble out b-o-o, and you might scroll to the get the correct auto-complete for the bookstore.

Conclusion

Thank you for making it through to the end of *Apple Watch: 101 Helpful Tips and Secret Tricks*. Let's hope it was informative and able to provide you with all of the tools you need to achieve your goals whatever they may be.

The latest in smart wearable technology from Apple has put competitors on notice. FitBit, Huawei, and Samsung have been putting out smartwatches that rival, but do not yet exceed, the all-around capabilities and ease of what the titans of tech have thus far created. The Apple Watch Series 3 is jam-packed with features that finally run fast and, with the advent of Apple Watch's cellular capability, can follow your day without letting you miss a beat.

More than 35 million smartwatches are expected to be purchased by the end of 2018, finally signaling that the wearable device is here to stay as a main player in the tech market. Make sure you make the most out of your Apple Smart Watch by learning all the nooks and cranny features which separate the casual user from the informed citizen. By understanding the core relationship between Apple Watch 3 and its iPhone platform, you can circumvent delays and frustration by streamlining the functionality of your watch.

You can set up the preferences and connectivity to extend your battery life (one of the few setbacks of the Apple series). After getting a grip (and Force Touch) on how to navigate your wearable tech, you can unleash the little device's powerful secrets to improve your life. Hack your communication, your fitness, your time management, and most importantly, go have fun!

The 101 Helpful Tips and Secret Tips guidebook turns the stop-and-go smartwatch experience into the seamless, 360-degree iLife that Apple promised since 2015. The price of the Apple Watch is already an investment. Make sure you match that investment with the priceless understanding of knowing you are getting the most benefits out of your tech buck.

Finally, if you found this book useful in any way, a review on Amazon is always appreciated!

Made in the USA
Lexington, KY
27 November 2018